Notes from the Shallow End – the stories that lie behind, beyond and somewhere in between the songs of the album "Drowning in the Shallow"

©Andy Flannagan 2012
Illustrated and Designed by Lloyd Kinsley

Published by Downwardly Mobile Music
www.andyflan.com

THE FOLLOWING ARE THE STORIES THAT
LIE BEHIND, BEYOND AND SOMEWHERE IN
BETWEEN THE SONGS ON MY ALBUM CALLED
"DROWNING IN THE SHALLOW".

YOU HAVEN'T HEARD THE ALBUM?

WELL THIS IS AWKWARD

AT GIGS, PEOPLE SEEM TO LOVE HEARING THE STORIES BEHIND THE SONGS. IT SEEMS TO HELP THEM INHABIT THE SONGS, AND BE ABLE TO FEEL ALL THE MORE STRONGLY WHAT I WAS FEELING WHEN I WROTE THEM. SO WE THOUGHT, LET'S TRY TO MAKE THAT HAPPEN WHEN PEOPLE AREN'T AT A GIG.

VOILA.

I HOPE IT'S USEFUL.

We live in a fast, flat world.

Technology is enabling us to fit more and more into our busy lives. We can now listen to music as we jog, read our emails on the bus, check headlines or sports results as we walk, or text our friends while we queue in a supermarket. The space to just be living, thinking and breathing is being squeezed out, sacrificed in the headlong pursuit of making our lives more efficient and entertained.

DOES THIS ACTUALLY MAKE OUR LIVES HAPPIER OR MORE EFFECTIVE?

Does this technology drive us to only look at what is in our immediate gaze on flat screens of various descriptions, never seeing beyond to the depth of what life and relationships have to offer? Is there a dimension that can't be measured by length, breadth or height? The reality is that even if this other dimension existed, we might not stop for long enough to see it or feel it. We instead opt for the safety of what we can touch, click or watch, missing out on the invisible adventure.

Will people look back on our generation in the same way that we look back on those who believed the earth was flat? The fact that so much of our sense of worth is hardwired to whether we are in any way reproduced on a flat screen (be that 'Facebook', 'YouTube', 'X-factor' or whatever), surely takes us into psychologically dangerous territory for the human race. My young nephew and niece have already seen themselves in more photographs in a few short years than I have in a whole life. I stand in gigs where people are busier taking photos or video than actually enjoying the experience. Or is this just a transition that every generation experiences? Would I have complained about the printing press too?

I stand in gigs where people are busier taking photos or video than actually enjoying the experience.

WIDE AND SHALLOW

In his book, "The Shallows" Nicholas Carr has highlighted some of the challenges of screen-centred living. It is a shallow world we inhabit when we accrue more and more DVDs, more and more mp3s, more and more friends on Facebook, yet fail to truly appreciate any of them. As a result, we lose the delight of gift and the truth of people and places being precious. We cover more and more holiday locations: – "Have you done Italy?" "Have you done Egypt?" ticking off our boxes. We flit around consuming, choosing from a thousand options, but never really digging deeper

into one story, one song, one friendship or one place. The constant stimulation of 'the new'- the curse of novelty – sometimes keeps us from knowing our roots, or ourselves. TV talent shows have such a pull on so many people because we crave the next big thing. They are marketed perfectly.

I have watched children gorge themselves on multiple birthday presents in a feast of functionality, working their way through ten or more presents in the space of mere minutes. Where is the awe that comes from stopping to appreciate?

WHERE IS THE WONDER? WHERE IS THE SENSE THAT LIFE IS A GIFT AND NOT A RIGHT?

Nicholas Carr's research has shown that our brains are actually changing as a result of our internet and screen dependency. Whole areas once exercised are being left to atrophy like the long-forgotten muscles of those who used to play sport regularly, but now just can't find the time or energy.

Let me give you an example. I confess I am writing this in the car as my wife drives us to her parents' house. (No multi-tasking irony there then!) Every few moments I want to swap windows on my laptop because I have become so used to the distraction of the immediate. The new email. The new text. Sitting in the car without Wi-Fi means I can't succumb to this simple disaster, but the experience is making me aware of how "wired" I've become. On a normal day in the office or at home, I often allow myself to be tripped up by any little new communication by email, text, Facebook, or phone, rather than staying on course with the deeper creative thing I need to do that day. Novelty trumps significance.

This became painfully clear when I did a 48 hour sponsored silence (fasting from all connectivity) last

year. I was forced to dig deep into reserves long since forgotten. I was forced to stop and think. I was even forced to pray.

Our tendencies became even clearer last year during the riots in the UK. It was the first ever revolution designed to ensure that the next revolution would be recorded in higher definition. Pocket-based fantastic gadgets were the prime looting target for a generation that on average already has 7 hours of 'screen time' per day. Last year's TV play "15 Million Merits" by Charlie Brooker was a scarily prophetic look into our potential future, where all of life is mediated via screens.

DON'T GET ME WRONG. TECHNOLOGY CAN BE WONDERFULLY USEFUL.

It is catalysing revolutions and calling governments and corporations to account. It is helping me create this. It probably let you know that this album was available. However, like all good gifts, when overused or misused it can cause serious problems. Like when we remove real relationships from economics or sex – financial crises and emotional carnage respectively.

HI-CARB DIET

I used to spend a lot of time highlighting to people that they need to watch and read the news with sensitive filters on their eyes and ears. I wanted to make clear that news corporations have a vested interest in printing what is tragic and scandalous, since they need to sell ads and papers to keep profits high. I wanted to remind people that what they were reading in any given context was far from the whole story.

They won't be reading too much good news, and they won't be reading about the wonderful but unremarked-upon acts of kindness and service that happen in communities up and down the country every day. The net effect is that we all become more cynical, depressed and unable to believe that positive change can occur. Because of my work in politics, I spent a lot of time encouraging folks to be involved in the media, to bring higher standards of journalism and a desire to tell the whole truth.

Now I still believe those things to be true, but I think there is also something more fundamental going on. We have allowed "news" to become the default information source for our lives. In some ways the "news" can't help it. It is "new". By its very definition it is novelty-based. However, novelty is a bit like carbohydrate: very necessary, but if your diet consists mostly of it, then you are in big trouble.

It is great for snacking to give you a quick hit, but long-term leaves you hugely undernourished if it is not part of a more varied diet. Our "incoming data" diet should surely include some ancient, deeper writing and art. It takes more effort and patience for sure, but there is huge reward in embracing what has stood the test of time, whether in the realm of music, philosophy or everywhere in between.

WE CONFUSE WHAT IS NEW FOR WHAT IS TRUE.

If my frame of reference for what is important or significant is based on a daily diet of the BBC news website (and it is much better than most!), then my plumb line is more like a pendulum. So this little package of book and CD is intentionally designed to be enjoyed slowly and I hope it draws on some ancient truth. Take a few hours to read and to listen. Be here now, and nowhere else. **Sit and read, sit and listen, and let what deep inside you, you know to be true, connect with you.** Let long-forgotten memories return. Let a snapshot of a future that is perfect enchant you and entice you. There is little hope to be found in the painstaking analysis of only what we can see. So turn the TV off, tune out the immediate, and listen to the ancient and future cries that bring meaning and purpose to life.

Please know - these are not the scribblings of someone who has this stuff nailed. I am regularly stuck in the shallow end.

As the ancient Chinese proverb goes, "He with 3000 Facebook friends should not throw stones".

I hope you don't mind some company on the journey.

May you be downwardly mobile so the depth of your life might increase.

DROW
NING
IN THE
SHAL
LOW

I lived in Luton for 7 years.
I loved it. Honest.

 I loved the people (and the excellent transport links!) For quite a while, however, there was something in my gut telling me that I needed to be in London to get more involved in politics. I really didn't want to leave my Luton life, with a fantastic group of friends, a strong sense of locality, and a great cricket team.

 I knew I had to go, but boy did I procrastinate. I kept dipping my toe in the water, but fear of the unknown and fear of failure kept me running back up the beach. During the same period of my life I was doing a lot of swimming, and I realised that especially when in the sea, I felt like I was doing something I was born to do. The sensation of motion with my hands crisply cutting the surface of the water was glorious, but there were many times that I just couldn't be bothered getting out to the deep water, even though I knew that it was a place where I would feel truly alive. That place was the less comfortable place. You know what it's like – you can have a paddling experience of the sea without actually getting into the sea.

GETTING OUT DEEP IS MUCH MORE AWKWARD.

For a start, you have to do that embarrassing changing beneath a towel thing that I just can't master. Then in the UK the water is generally freezing cold. Then you have those key pain barriers – the water up to your ankles (okay), then your knees(colder), your nether regions(eeeeesh), then your shoulders(deep breath), then the head(brain freeze). Then that salty water gets into your eyes and nostrils. Am I selling it to you well? For me, though, it is all worth it for those moments just a few minutes later, when your body has acclimatised to the ridiculous temperature.

At that point something in me feels connected to the wild sea and the beauty of creation – I realise I am an independent, yet so dependent creature

 Yet getting to that place of challenge means conquering some fears and being prepared for a level of discomfort that the world trains us to avoid. For too long I settled for the comfortable and the familiar. I am obviously a slow learner, because this wasn't the first time that I had been reminded that my fear of failure (and losing control) was holding me back from experiencing life in all its fullness.

In the days before mobile phones, I had arrived somewhere in the Mourne Mountains in Northern Ireland to meet my sister, but unbeknownst to me, she was unable to come. I sat waiting, parked in full view of these beautiful rolling fields stretching back up a mountainside. However I was confused as to why the farmer had planted two different shades of grass. Some areas were bright green and some were dark green. I became even more confused when the different areas began moving. My fears of temporary insanity were relieved when I finally realised that it was the clouds that were moving overhead!

D'OH!

My imagination continued to run however, and I could see myself as a little ant jumping around on the grass, always making sure I was in the bright green area. As soon as the shadow began to encroach, I would hop off to another bright section. I was learning about my life. I was going out of my way to make sure that I was spending time where it was bright – i.e. where the popular people hung out, where I

As soon as things became a bit awkward, I would ship off to find some excitement or comfort elsewhere.

felt comfortable, where exciting things were happening, where things were going well. As soon as things became a bit awkward, I would ship off to find some excitement or comfort elsewhere. 'Am I called to that?' I thought, or am I called to stand still – to stand with people in their bright times and in their dark times, to share their joys and their sufferings? The writer Henri Nouwen wrote that a crucial part of life is 'displacement'. By displacement he meant deliberately putting yourself in a situation where you would not naturally be. A place where you might not be totally comfortable. We learn so much about others, about ourselves and I believe about our creator, when we displace ourselves, crossing boundaries to leave what is

familiar and safe territory. You may only need to go 3 streets away to experience that sense of displacement.

This, however, is horrendously difficult in 21st century life because we have all developed finely tuned 'suffering avoidance mechanisms' that kick in when we see even a hint of effort coming around the corner. When we intentionally remove ourselves from hard places, we are limiting our growth, as well as the impact that we could be having on a hurting world. It is an interesting exercise to analyse our life decisions in an attempt to get to the actual values that are informing them. I'm thinking of decisions such as which area of a town to live in, what size of a car to drive, and what type of people we spend social time with. For me the values that often inform those decisions are the prime drivers of our society – namely comfort and safety. We said we would look to history for inspiration, and interestingly those aren't the values I see fleshed out in the life of Jesus Christ.

He had a pretty high-risk, low-security existence, where the questions were not all about how to avoid awkward situations, but how to turn them on their head to signpost a better way - where the last came first and the first came last. He was walking proof that the hope we all want to see brought to the world doesn't come without sacrifice. Warm fuzzy feelings just won't do it.

That's where the last verse of the song springs from really. Resurrection isn't possible without crucifixion. Think of a seed – it needs to be utterly dead before it can explode into life. New life isn't possible without the death of the stuff that stops us truly living.

It's also why a baptism can sometimes look like a drowning.

DROWNING IN THE SHALLOW

I would plant my feet
where angels fear to tread,
But I am treading water,
and feeling like I'm dead.

Failure is my fear,
and caution is my call,
But the surest way to
sink is when you
don't move at all.

Fall down, would you fall
down on me, Fall down

I've been drowning in the
shallow, Stuck waiting for the
rainbow, But it's only when I
swim I feel alive

I have had enough of
this obvious sin,
Playing for a draw when
there's a guaranteed win.

Now I think I understand
what all of this involves.
Comfort's calling me to
back to the sand.
'Cos this sea is killing me,
but I know I'm free.

So lead me to your depths
Immerse me gently there
'Cos freedom comes
from dying,
Then coming up for air.

Words and Music: Andy Flannagan ©2008
Downwardly Mobile Music

I meet so many people, young men in particular, who spend much of their twenty-something lives asking the questions, "Why am I here?", "What am I meant to be doing with my life?" and, "Who am I meant to be doing it with?"

So much angst and energy is spent seeking out the "right" path and the "right" partner. It feels as if folks are staring at a map of the world and desperately trying to work out exactly where they should place a pin. You get the sense that if that pin is as much as a millimetre away from the exact point where it is meant to be, then it could be disastrous. Or at least there is a presumption that you could miss out on what has been "planned".

My fear is that we all spend so much of our lives trying to work out the specifics of what we are "destined for" or "called to", that we miss the obvious stuff that we are all called to. There is such emotional investment in finding "the answer" that we miss the importance of fleshing out what we do know to be true – the non-negotiables that come without question marks attached.

The 'what am I meant to be doing?' question was famously asked by the Old Testament prophet Micah in the form, "What does the Lord require of you?" He lived in complex times of poverty and oppression in many ways not dissimilar to ours. The end of the 8th century BC was panic-filled for the people of Judah, with the Assyrians preparing to invade. Finding the needle of destiny in the haystack, even when you were trying to do the right thing, would have been challenging. Micah could have found many justifications for just looking after number one. I believe, though, Micah's answer to his own question "What does the Lord require of you?" rings out across the centuries as a simple call.

"ACT JUSTLY, LOVE MERCY AND WALK HUMBLY WITH YOUR GOD."

This simplicity of focus would surely change many of our lives. The shocking truth that life is more about HOW we do it than WHAT we do in it is often troubling to me. Am I in the "right" job? Are we living in the "right" area? I would rather be right about where I'm meant to be and what I'm meant to be doing and then not have to worry much more about how I do it. That way I can relax and not be annoyed by constant ethical decisions. I fool myself that I might someday reach the distant horizon of 'sortedness,' where everything will be in place. I then expend huge amounts of energy trying to control all the variables of my life to get there.

However, that's not the life that Micah is talking about. He was calling his listeners to daily flesh out justice, mercy and humility in whatever situation they found themselves in. What if our simpler destiny was to become more fully human, displaying these incredible, and world-changing, traits of justice, mercy and humility? Could that simultaneously increase our motivation and decrease our stress levels?

Perhaps another part of the problem is that we have become so ruthlessly functional. Our lives are centred on what we do rather than who we are. The first question at a party is almost always, "So what do you do?" If what we do is a primary decider of worth

or status then it is not surprising that we invest so much effort in "doing the right thing".

Simplicity is what our hearts, souls and minds crave, but we rarely allow them to get close to it. There is a huge freedom in just trying to love the people around you. That is one of the reasons my wife Jen and I are desperately trying to be downwardly mobile. To eat and drink simply. To put boundaries on our "screen time". To hang out with not just the folks we like the most. To make a statement to ourselves at least, if not the world, that increasing power and influence is not necessarily found by ascending the career and social ladders that have been prescribed for us. We need constant reminders that change doesn't always come from the top down. If you happen to be someone trying to follow the man called Jesus, then you're called to

There is a huge freedom in just trying to love the people around you.

have friends in all the wrong places as well as the right ones. In fact in his day it was a primary criticism of the way he went about his life.

I have been so inspired by some incredible people who have followed that example and moved themselves and their families into tough estates or even slums to try and bring a bit of hope and life. One crew are called 'Urban Neighbours of Hope' – **www.unoh.org** You can read many of their amazing stories online.

He found a Bible in a drawer, fell in love with the Jesus he read about ...

One of them is a Kiwi called Mick Duncan. I heard him tell his story at a conference in Melbourne. He was a drug dealer until the day he was taken into someone's home, having been found lying in the street in a drug-induced haze. He found a Bible in a drawer, fell in love with the Jesus he read about, and desperately wanted to tell others about his new friend. Reading of Christ's heart for the poor, he then went to live and work in the slums of Manila for 10 years.

The most profound moment of his presentation, however, came when he invited his youngest daughter up to share the stage with him. She commented that her friends in New Zealand always asked, "So what was it like living amongst all that poverty?" She said that her response was simply, "I didn't see any poverty. I just saw my friends." Wow. You could hear a pin drop, and more than a few tears. I thought, "Could we become the generation for whom that is true? A generation whose children won't have to start charities to alleviate poverty, because they will simply be helping their neighbours as friends."

When Mick took the microphone back off his daughter, he spoke of how his eldest son was now working in one of the toughest, drug and crime-infested estates of Wellington.

HE SPOKE WITH TEARFUL PRIDE. IT WAS A GLORIOUSLY COUNTER-CULTURAL MOMENT.

A father was on a stage beaming with pride because his son was living in the worst place possible. What an inversion of the desperation that we feel to impress family and friends with the size of our houses, or the areas we live in.

... he then went to live and work in the slums of Manila for 10 years.

The tripartite magnetic fields of justice, mercy and humility tug us in directions that we would not otherwise want to go, yet ensure that when we get there (and along the way), we don't forget who we are and why we're there. We remember that our help is not needed, but wanted.

We remember that when the marginalised are our friends and neighbours we may not need expensive and complicated programmes to see change. We remember that the love of money is the root of all kinds of evil (what a huge statement!). We remember that there is right and wrong. We remember that we regularly get it wrong.

The call to simple living is one that is hard to follow because every other message from newspapers to advertising, to the internet, to TV is screaming, "Become MORE significant. Then you will be happy.

Get a bigger website. Gain more influence and impact. Earn more money. Have more stuff. Have more friends."

We can't 'live simply' by just hoping to paddle upstream against the tide. We need to make some conscious decisions that will constrain us (yes constrain us) to be face to face with people in need regularly. We can't do it on our own. Transformation comes through groups of people who have promised to stick with each other and stick to some rhythms of living counter-culturally; and that transformation cuts both ways. We learn and are changed in the process of giving ourselves.

These rhythms could be the 21st century equivalent of the Old Testament laws like Jubilee, where land was to be given back to its original owners after forty-nine years. These laws were based on God's wise presumption that left to their own devices, within the nation of Israel power and wealth would accumulate in the hands of the few. It's so good to know we've come such a long way from that haven't we? The tide of human self-centredness inevitably flows that way, and I am no different. I need rhythms that remind me life is a gift and not a right. I need rhythms that remind me that I am not the centre of the universe. Otherwise I default to my own comfort and security. Multiply me by 7 billion and you get the reason why the global economic system is making the rich richer and the poor poorer.

So what about putting some groove in your life? Like any drummer will tell you, it takes a lot of discipline to learn a rhythm and stick to it, but once you do it provides the spine to be able to do lots of other fun things. The discipline actually brings freedom, and it means lots of other people can play with you too. Some of us try to play music without a stable rhythm. Sometimes our 'organic spontaneity' is just selfish noise.

What rhythms might get you more regularly where you need to be and with whom you need to be, to help get your heart to where it needs to be?

WHAT ABOUT?

♡ Binning your TV aerial. (you can still catch stuff on the internet if you really need to, but at least you control it, rather than it controlling you?)
♡ Moving to an area which is in need of some hope.
♡ Seeking out any excuse to throw parties.
♡ Eating with your neighbours once every couple of weeks.
♡ Once a week, living off just £5 for the day.
♡ Only eating meat at weekends.
♡ Taking 10 minutes every day to be absolutely still and silent.

Living. Simple. Not really.

THE REASON

While you're waiting, the blonde
have been leading the blind
While you're watching, the wound
teach us how to unwind
Finding needles in haystacks,
falling in lust, or rags to riches
Always looking for subplots but
never the thrust of simple living

This is the reason
that you're here -
You've always known it.
This is the reason
that you're here -
So go on and own it.
This is the reason
that you're here -
But leading's lonely
This is the reason
that you're here.

While you're waiting, the rich
have been raping the poor
While you're watching,
their bricks have been
made out of straw
Signing over your conscience
to free market lies -
this trickle tickle
Getting downwardly mobile
opens your eyes to really living

Would you stop
looking for clues?
This is no mystery.

Act justly, love mercy, walk
humbly with your God.

Words and Music: Andy Flannagan -
©2008 Downwardly Mobile Music

PIECES
OF **APRIL**

I have met so many young people who have broken my heart while telling me the stories of their broken lives.

Many of them were from Luton. Often through no fault of their own they were left growing up in situations that were physically, emotionally and spiritually less than ideal.

While on holiday in Norfolk a crew of us from Luton watched the movie "Pieces of April". In it, an estranged daughter played by Katie Holmes is desperately trying to piece together a family 'Thanksgiving' dinner with very limited resources. This will probably be their last ever 'Thanksgiving' together, as her mum is dying of cancer. Her relationship with her mum is however totally dysfunctional for a variety of reasons. In scene after scene you observe the heart-wrenching effects of this fragmentation. Afterwards I just went to my bedroom and cried. The broken relationships represented in it and their knock-on effects were such strong echoes of the same reality in Luton

AS I SAT CRYING, A SCENE FLASHED INTO MY HEAD. IT WAS OF A JIGSAW PUZZLE WHOSE PIECES WERE SCATTERED ALL OVER A FLOOR.

That is normally a positive, exciting moment, filled with the anticipation of things coming together. However, this scene was darker. The box in which the pieces had resided had been carelessly tossed away.

Young people of the 21st century are often left trying to put the pieces together without the photo or picture of how they all fit together. They don't have a big picture or a big story that makes sense of and gives context to their little story. They sense, though, that the pieces are meant to fit together somehow so they instinctively make it up as they go along, forcing pieces together. They then have to rip them apart again when it becomes clear that it maybe isn't just that easy without a reference point. Even more hurt and pain can then ensue. Many haven't been provided with that framework because of physically or emotionally absent parents. For many more, no-one has told them that there is a big story. Surely part of our job is to give back the box.

This broken picture sometimes leads people to give up on a whole generation, but we mustn't lose track of a deeper truth as we cry over the wreckage of broken lives. I think there is hope. And it comes from knowing where we fit in the big picture. I believe we are all made in the image of God.

I BELIEVE WE ALL HAVE THE STUFF OF GOD IN US. HE MADE US A BIT LIKE HIM.

WE CARRY DIVINE DNA.

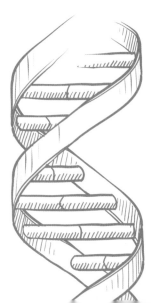

Stop and wonder about that for a moment. Even if you don't believe there is a God, never mind a human race made in his image, you would surely agree that we have some inbuilt goodness. You can insert that thought for the rest of this if you need to!

The problem is that being an image-bearer is not the first thing we think when we look at ourselves in the mirror. We physically and metaphysically first look to our blemishes, forgetting the core of who we are. Over the years, through hurts inflicted on us, through bad decisions we make, that image becomes blurred or cracked or covered in dust, like an old painting that has been forgotten in the attic. But that image is still innately there, and the pieces can be put back together.

CREATIVITY

This holds true even in extreme scenarios. I will never forget my first morning visiting Castington Young Offenders' institution. About fifteen lads paraded in with the classic "hard" exterior, keen to let me know that I was on their turf, and that we would be playing by their rules! We were encouraging them to take part in a rap workshop. At the end of the week they would perform the rap that they had written to the other inmates.

CAREFULLY PLACED VERBAL DARTS CAME MY WAY FOR THE FIRST FEW MINUTES AS THEY JOCKEYED FOR POSITION WITH THE 'NEW BOY'.

Then I was met with looks of utter disbelief as they realised that this strange Irish guy was actually suggesting that they could create something worthwhile and that others would listen to it! The beginning of the process was as hard as not just getting blood out of a stone, but also transfusing it into some bodies close to death! I encouraged the lads to be brutally honest about how they were feeling. They had a chance to vent all their frustrations at "the system". It quite literally was "Rage against the machine". That rage was usually being directed at other inmates, wardens and walls. Their first drafts painted a dark, but honest picture of the inside of their cells and more importantly the inside of their heads and hearts.

I suggested that instead of expressing their annoyance at some generic "system" which seemed more like a nebulous fog, why not express their annoyance to someone who might actually be listening and might actually respond? Why not address these words to God? They were surprised that I wanted to expose God to that sort of verbal battery. "Don't worry, I said – he's big enough to handle himself." The next day the lads came back

and the change in dynamic was palpable. Something had happened. It was all still very angry and honest, and the lyrics mightn't be suitable for printing here, but there was a reflection in the tone and content that hadn't been there before.

After the first lad finished, I said, "Well done mate, you've just written your first Psalm."

"What? No way, no I haven't. No", he blurted as he stepped back in surprise.

Later I read them some of David's angrier work from the Bible (which makes up a good proportion of his work!), and they started to see what I meant, nodding their heads in agreement. By getting creative they were connecting with their creative creator. I believe they were exercising the creative spark placed in them by the one in whose image they were made. An inevitable connection is made when you do that. A link is forged (even if it's only subconscious) when a child does something that they have seen their parents doing. And in the prison, not only was that creative connection occurring, they were actually communicating with words. Whether they liked it or not, they were praying. It may have been a modest start, but a real relationship was beginning. A relationship based on honest communication. We all know that those are the relationships that last, rather than the ones where we're pretending, simply saying all the right things at the right time.

ID CARDS

So, if you truly believe that every human being you interact with is a carrier of the image of God, does that not change how you interact with them? To quote Vinoth Ramachandrara, when you stand face to face with another human being, you are standing in the presence of, "A vehicle of the divine". Does that affect how you treat the cleaner at your school, or the young person hunched on your street corner, or the guy behind the counter at McDonalds, or the lady working in the call centre?

Try an experiment for me. Keep a postcard in your pocket (you could call it an ID card!) On it make an attempt to note down what you see of the image of God or some innate goodness in every person that you meet in the next 24 hrs (especially the young people). It may be their gentle smile – it may be their perseverance with an ailing relative – it may be their sporting prowess. Write these things down. The day I spent doing this changed the way I look at people. It shamed me. I can be so quick to criticise and so slow to spot goodness. The trouble is that if I struggle to recognise the image of God in myself, the chances are I won't be looking for it too closely in anyone else. We love to critique. We love to presume the worst as at least we can rest content in the useless cosiness that we are slightly better than someone else.

To get back to those jigsaw pieces. It is a beautiful thing when they do come together, but as I write I have just been told that an old friend from Luton has committed suicide. Nobody knew anything was wrong.

AGAIN, WE ARE MORE BROKEN THAN WE KNOW. IN THE MOVIE, THERE IS HOWEVER A BEAUTIFUL MOMENT OF RESTORATION AND RECONCILIATION OF THAT FAMILY, AND MY HOPE IS NO DIFFERENT FOR THE MANY OTHERS WHOSE LIVES ARE STILL A CONFUSING PUZZLE.

PIECES OF APRIL

Running from
A ghost that's gone.
The secret arena where you
fight yourself is filling up now.
The Romans are baying
for your soul.
So pledge your allegiance
to a flag
that flies above the earth now,
'Cos two halves don't
make you whole.

These pieces of April
Betray her smiling face.
These fragments of dreaming
Are scattered into space.
And if time is a healer,
He's run right out of grace.
But these pieces of April
Will one day find their place.

You tipped her out,
But left her without
The picture upon her
box to hold onto

When all is changing,
The true horizon for her heart.
She's left with a puzzle
with no end in sight,
Where it's easier to
hide than fall apart.

Now I don't know
when this pain will end,
And I don't know if you
will face it again.
So would you let
this love enfold you?
And would you let
this love remould you?
Would you speak
those words unspoken?
Would you now believe
you're broken?

Words and Music: Andy Flannagan -
©2009 Downwardly Mobile Music

EGO

Do you agree or disagree with the following statement?

☐ *Agree*　　　　☐ *Disagree*

Love without promises isn't really love.

I think I am learning this stuff slowly. In 2008 I was in Australia doing some concerts. Jen and I had been going out for about 4 months. I was missing her in a pretty major way. My suspicion that she was the woman I was going to marry was being confirmed. In fact, I was already plotting and scheming the purchase of a shiny gold thing at the end of my time in Melbourne! However, Jen was going through some really difficult stuff back home that had taken both her and me by surprise. Our distance apart and the intensity of the issue combined to knock me sideways. This woman who I was about to

commit to for life was surprisingly not perfect, (I don't think she'd mind me saying that!) and neither was I. I was realising I could not protect her from everything, especially her past, and that it would inevitably have an impact on me too. The potential for much future pain was right in front of my eyes. Tears came easily, both lovingly for her situation and selfishly for mine.

Sitting on my bed, freezing cold in the Australian winter, the truth of what I was stepping into, and why it was important, became very clear. The reality of what love means was made plain to me. Love equals sacrifice. I misuse the word 'love' so regularly. I say things like, "I love doing that", implying that love equates with simply feeling good about something. If love is just a positive feeling (even in extremis) then it can fade pretty fast when I don't enjoy x, y or z anymore. We overuse and undersell this most amazing word. That's why I said love without promises really isn't love. For much of my life, my way of avoiding hassle and effort was to pull back from intimacy. The escape clause was always there. Now the promise that I was intending to make to Jen was leaving me no wiggle room. I could almost smell something burning!

Love is putting yourself second, and sometimes last, and that can really hurt.

In a world where we are trained to organise every detail to suit ourselves best, it can come as quite a shock. I have myspace, my documents and my pictures, and woe betide anyone who should mess with those. We live in a narcissistic iPod age, where individualising and owning everything is assumed as the sign of a fulfilled, self-sufficient life. For example, rather than do the hard work of understanding, negotiation, and compromise, we simply put a TV in everybody's bedroom. We have believed the lie that our role in life is to be consumers, and that increased choice brings us increased pleasure. It doesn't. In fact it often paralyses us. And worse than that, it trains us in getting exactly what we want, which makes us less rather than more human. But that is a tough lesson to learn, and it was extremely tough for me to narrow all the options down to just one. However, I'm so glad I did.

I am starting to see that the secrets of sacrifice can only be learned in intentional community, where habits at first begrudgingly undertaken eventually lead our hearts into preferring others for

FRIENDS = AUDIENCE
STATUS UPDATE = PRESS RELEASE

real. Marriage is just one example of such a community!

So why not ask yourself - who am I allowing close enough to rub off my rough edges? Who is pulling my thoughts away from me to make me less selfish? Who have I committed to, or promised to be there for, to leave me no wiggle room? Promises are hard to keep, but they lead to being more fully human. Are there neighbours you should be hanging out with? Is there stuff you should be sharing rather than purchasing?

ALTAR :EGO

Alongside all the above I am slowly realising that my ego inflates when even the slightest gap appears between who I truly am and who I present myself to be. You're only as honest as your last 'Facebook' status update. The online social media phenomenon means that we have all become our own press officers, selecting and spinning what makes it out into the public realm. For "Friends" read "audience." For "Status update" read "Press release." Some of us don't pretend that it's 'real'. We use it to publicise things and scavenge for ideas to a wide clientele that few believe are "real-world-equivalent" friends. We dip in and out, having had the benefit of building relationships normally for years. It is more of a flirtation (but still a potentially dangerous and time-wasting one) than a marriage. However, I do reckon that we are potentially betraying the generations that follow us.

AS OF 2012,
THERE ARE
500 MILLION
ACTIVE
FACEBOOK
USERS.
APPROX.
1 IN EVERY
13 PEOPLE
ON EARTH.

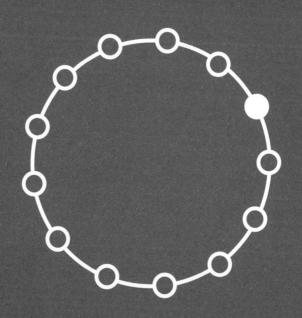

The problem is that many young people are growing into this as their main means of interaction, having not known anything different. Throw in the increasingly and disturbingly visual weighting of online media and you have all the ingredients you need for a generation of public image obsessed folks who have lost contact with anything deeper than a screen.

So take the scary reality of celebrity lifestyle and psychology as it is now: - the constant need to be on screen, in the papers, or on the web to build up "currency". The obsession with body shape. The disintegration of normal social interaction with those who used to be friends or family. The inability to say what you feel for fear of how it will be perceived. The separation of reality and fantasy and the corresponding dependency on alcohol and drugs for escapism. These celebrity afflictions are there for all to see.

What I fear is that if we continue to be our own press officers, eyes looking permanently over shoulders, becoming more and more image-obsessed, then these celebrity traits will be the sad state of affairs for a good chunk of the population, not just the celebrities. Are we already halfway there? Talk to any youth worker about the anxiety levels and depression they encounter.

A NEW GENERATION MAY NEVER KNOW THE SAFE SPACE OF REAL FRIENDSHIPS WHERE HONESTY AND HEALING ARE POSSIBLE. LET'S TRY TO MODEL AT LEAST A FEW.

EGO

I've tried to follow
I've often failed
I've tried to swallow
This bitter pill
I'll take the glory
But skip the pain
Edit the story
To fit my frame

And now my shame has
me sparring for a fight
This town ain't big enough
for me and me tonight

My ego's on the altar now
Escaping through the
flames somehow

I took so long to realise
That loving equals sacrifice

I'm left defending
These hollow wins
But this trip is ending
Where freedom begins

And now my fear leaves
one more unfinished song
I'll hide in here till the critics'
pens have gone.

Words and Music: Andy Flannagan -
©2010 Downwardly Mobile Music

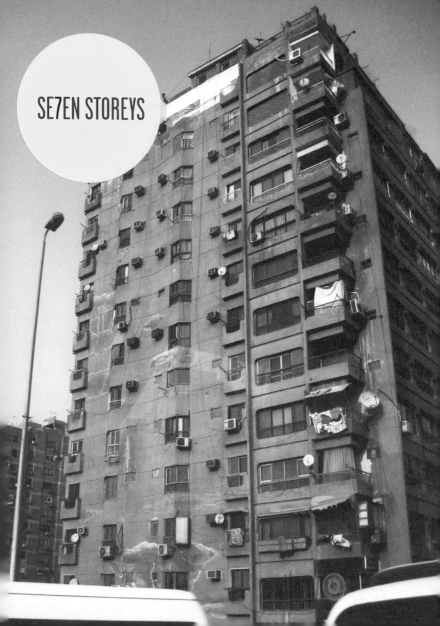

SE7EN STOREYS

There are some stories you simply don't want to tell, because they are too horrendous. But they often must be told.

While we were in Cairo recently Jen and I were invited for dinner to the apartment of an Egyptian family. As you can imagine, the hospitality was incredible. It was a joyous evening, full of great food and laughter, often at my fumbled attempts at speaking Arabic. Our hosts were very patient!

They spoke at length of the challenges of living as Christians in a majority Muslim nation. One of the ladies recounted many stories of the discrimination she experienced on a daily basis on public transport, at work, or simply in the street. Verbal insults and spitting were commonplace. However nothing prepared us for hearing the story of their friend from the same apartment block. On the seventh floor lived a lady called Nadia who because of their care and kindness had started to ask questions about their faith. She started to secretly attend their church, and became a Christian. However as with so many people like her (an estimated half million people in Egypt) she kept her new faith hidden from her family, as conversion to Christianity from Islam often carries unbearable consequences, especially for women.

This carried on for some months until things got to the point where Nadia could not keep the news from her husband, wanting to share with him the reason why her life felt transformed for the better.

I could try to prolong this story with much detail, milking the drama, but I won't. One evening, she told her husband what had

No religion can claim a monopoly on victimhood

happened, and he threw her to her death from the apartment's seventh floor balcony. After dinner I walked out to our hosts' identical balcony four floors below. I stared up and then down to the ground, churning the reality around in my head and guts. I had heard similar stories before, but I had never been in the neighbourhood.

Sadly history shows us that no religion can claim a monopoly on victimhood. The experience reminded me that shame and fear are huge, potentially explosive things. Only meaningful relationships can build bridges with others whose lives and faith we do not understand, and may therefore fear. A Northern Irishman like me sadly knows that in the vacuum of a lack of contact, untruth and prejudice have fertile ground to grow.

The political transition that began not long after our trip brings both huge opportunities and challenges. The atmosphere was summed up for me by one Egyptian who told us that it felt like they were living in a room full of gas, where at any moment, someone could strike a match. May the friction decrease.

SO THIS IS A SONG FOR NADIA, AND ALL HER BROTHERS AND SISTERS; BOTH MUSLIM AND CHRISTIAN.

SEVEN STOREYS

Seven storeys
Fall to glory
High minds stoop so low

Fear is the fist with
which you strike me
But you can't reach
to my dreams

Never will I regret this journey
For His love has conquered fear

I can not be silent
So you silence me

No space for my new faith
So I die

Words: Andy Flannagan, Music: Andy
Flannagan, Alan Branch, Dave Cooke
©2011 Downwardly Mobile Music

⑥ this poet

has left me without...

... words

Whether we like it or not, we are all products of someone else.

The modern world can fool us into believing that we are truly independent beings, cast free from the shackles of family and history, but the more I grow up, the more I realise I am the product of my parents. Happily that makes me smile broadly, as even though my bias is pretty huge, I believe them to be the best parents in the world!

Their love and support for me has been unstinting, no matter what random decisions I have made. Their servant hearts and encouragement continue to amaze me, especially when I watch them interact with others, building community effortlessly. Things that I had presumed were impressiveness by me have been reassigned in my mind to "Aha – yes - I think I've nicked that from my dad/mum!" However, I know

many other people for whom that same smile is either forced, or an honest grimace. They have not known an encouraging, supportive context in which to grow up. Even if it has been a generally positive experience, there have been specific words, actions or a lack thereof, that have sowed lies deep into their understanding of who they are.

Understanding that our parents were themselves the products of their parents, and so on, back to our furthest ancestors, is however key to releasing them from our expectations of perfection. This is especially true when we are faced with the consequences of their questionable actions or inactions in our own lives. I honestly believe that there is a heartbreaking story behind every heartbreaking story; but I also believe that unconditional love can break cycles that have gone on for generations.

The song sprang from seeing the pain of a girl whose dad who didn't express in words that he was proud of her, that she was beautiful, or that he loved her. I cried as I observed how paralysing that vacuum was.

There are no immutable limitations on people no matter what context they grow up in, so this is an observation as opposed to a rule, but we operate at our best when we know the affirmation and security of loving parents. We'd love to think that we're stronger than that. We'd love to believe that we could become psychologically self-sufficient. Sadly many of us have no choice but to be so. But what is so painful to watch is the absence or shallowness of that parental connection when it could be present. For example watching all the dimensions of dad-replacement-therapy (or its reactive opposite) play out breaks my heart. It can involve high defences, knee-jerk response attacks, and self-preserving control of situations and relationships. Yet it is the most understandable thing. I wrote this once about someone I love dearly, "She longs to be free. She longs to not need him. But she does. She

longs for his applause, but chooses absence rather the possibility of silence. She sits crumpled in the wings, unaware that there is someone else standing applauding her in the 3rd seat of the 5th row, before she has even taken the stage. It's someone whose joy and appreciation is not dependent on her performance, but the fact that she is His daughter."

My cry to those who play a role in relationships of any kind – (be it friend, daughter, mother, son, father, or lover) – is to take a moment to let the other half know in words or actions how much they mean to you. Even if you're not feeling it overflowing out of you, you may need to (as my mate Dave Steell says) "fake it to make it" – the action of doing it makes the healthy reality more likely. Learn the script, as it may have been forgotten somewhere down the line in your family.

It was heartbreaking to be at the funeral of a 26-year-old recently, whose friends piled tributes on him in their eulogies. He had lived an abundant life that touched so many people. One was left thinking what impact these words would have had if they had been delivered while he was still alive. He committed suicide. We are not as strong as we think we are.

COPING

We all understand the need for physical healing, but often ignore the need for emotional healing. Like a nagging neck or back injury, some hurt (that we may not even recognise or remember) subconsciously impedes our ability to move and love freely. I used to think that people should, "just get over it", but I realise now that that denies the reality of how we are made. It is wonderful that we are made to feel things deeply. It means that we can experience deep joy, but it also means that we can experience serious pain. Too many of us have settled for the numbing analgesia of modern life that flattens out the highs so as not to cause a scene, and represses the lows so we can get through the day. We force them to a forgotten place until

The only times I stop trying to protect myself are when I know someone else is on it.

they jump out and grab us when we least expect it. Sometimes healing is fast, in a majestic whoosh, but often it is infuriatingly slow. My hope for me and everyone else is that in our impatience we don't settle for coping rather than healing. Often that healing is released by being able to forgive those who have hurt us, but the resources to do that rarely come from within.

The very fact that healing occurs in our physical selves is incredible. Our bodies are somehow able to fight off infections, cause skin to fuse to seal up cuts and grazes, flush out impurities, and send troops to places of injury (creating hilarious bruises) bringing the restoration of muscle and other tissue. Even bones fuse back together. Healing is an incredible thing when you stop to think about it. Generally in life we don't expect broken things to fix themselves, but our bodies do fix themselves.

However the resources for the healing don't all come from inside the body. The air we breathe, the water we drink, and the nutrients we ingest are all vital as fuel for the process. Similarly we need external, invisible help to make the journey from coping to healing. That's where the unconditional love from the guy standing applauding in 5th row comes in. His name would be Jesus. The only times I stop trying to protect myself are when I know someone else is on it.

To be healed is a wonderful, beautiful thing. I see it change faces, bodies and outlooks. I see it transform relationships, and I believe that one day 'Healing PLC' will be out of business, because there will be no more healing to be done.

BRING IT ON.

HEALING

These programmed
feelings leave you reeling
But you are not the cause, no.
This out-of-fashion
lack of passion
Has dignified what was.

This self-protection
stalls rejection,
And leaves you looking strong.
This piece of theatre
keeps things neater,
Pretending nothing's wrong.

Healing comes too
slow these days
I long to see you whole
Freedom's cornered

in this maze
Until you lose control.

I see you waiting,
all hope fading
Of hearing his applause.
But you're not hearing
someone cheering,
Who's seeing
through your flaws.

This cold front has
made you shiver
The chill has numbed
you to your core
How come? How long?

I love the TV series "The West Wing". I mean I really love it. I know I am not alone in this passion.

The scripts and characters are incredible, and that is a gloriously good thing. However this song is my confessional for all the times I have chosen fantasy over reality. For all the times I have chosen easy, controllable, fake relationships over the people next door. My neighbours are less glossy, less witty, and less good looking than anyone in the West Wing, but they're real.

We could all probably answer more quiz questions correctly about the lives of celebrities than about the lives of our actual neighbours. Our inbuilt desire to connect is still evident - we still want to know things about people, but often only if there is no possibility that they may need us at any point in time. That would require some sacrifice, and may cause our daily schedule to be disturbed. Happily, celebrities will never ask anything of us, except our unstinting devotion from a safe distance. Our fear of rejection also drives us towards those who will never reject us, but instead welcome us to their two-dimensional worlds.

To short-circuit our desires to vegetate, or merely hang out with people who are just the same as us, my wife Jen and I have "neighbour nights". Every fortnight we have one of our neighbours or their family group round for dinner. If we didn't schedule these in, then to be honest I don't know if they would happen. In London especially, there can be a tendency for your living space to be merely the place where you emerge from and come back to, but never welcome anyone else to. Much socialising happens in "third

Fact: Sidney Poitier was considered for the role of President Bartlet.

space" places like pubs and cafes. This can reduce the act of dwelling in a certain locality to an act of functionality, ignoring all the glory of the random strangers whom we have been thrown together with.

THERE IS A MAJOR PROBLEM WITH THE POST-MODERN ANALYSIS THAT COMMUNITIES OF SHARED INTEREST ARE REPLACING COMMUNITIES OF SHARED GEOGRAPHY.

I don't dispute that it is true, but I dispute that it represents progress. With the internet, it is now easier than ever to find other people exactly like you. Even in your subgroup of a niche within a subset, you can still find plenty of willing kin. However, continually hanging out with those who are like us means that we never develop the communication skills or conflict resolution skills to interact with those who are different than us. We therefore miss out on the inevitable learning and growth that occurs as social human beings. The perfect example of this is my homeland: Northern Ireland. Fear, ignorance and prejudice grow in the vacuum created by two peoples living in separate areas, and sometimes separate towns. Did you know that still only 5% of Northern Irish children are educated with children from the other side of the religious fence?

Another problem of 'communities of shared interest' trumping local communities is that there is now much reduced mixing between the 'haves' and 'have-nots', and even less between the 'haves' and

Fact: Martin Sheen's somewhat unusual way of putting his jacket on is caused by an injury to his arm sustained at birth.

Our brains are always on and we are inevitably products of what we expose them to.

'have-lots'. Our streets, estates and churches (or other faith groupings) are some of the only places left where people from vastly different socio-economic backgrounds can mix and learn from each other. If we restrict our socialising to those whom we work with or those whom we study with, there is a whole world that we are missing out on, and who are missing out on us. Even this opportunity is shrinking, as more and more areas become ghetto-ised, ethnically cleansing those on modest salaries or none.

If that wasn't enough, there are other challenges that emanate from our shallow, flat-screen dependencies. Before I get to them, I should say that the West Wing does inspire me to strive for excellence in anything I write. Aaron Sorkin's scripts have been described as symphonies, because of the beautifully hidden recurring themes, and precise signatures. But at the same time I don't know how many hours I have wasted in front of the TV, hiding from the challenges that I have been facing or avoiding creativity. "Hey we all need time to unwind and turn our brains off", we cry. Except we can't turn our brains off. Our brains are always on and we are inevitably products of what we expose them to. 'Garbage in, garbage out' goes the famous phrase, and TV today is very much quantity not quality!

Reading before going to bed has been proven to help you sleep. It's called "fictive rest,", using up our creative energies to imagine worlds, leaving us tired enough to sleep. Watching TV has the opposite effect, stimulating all our visual sensors directly, leaving a trail of neurones still firing long after we have laid our heads on our pillows. It is not a recipe for real rest, or real peace.

Watching TV, for me, is like treading water for the soul. The very act seems to say life is about hanging on in there until the end, just surviving. Watching TV will kill a few more hours until my inevitable demise. I have no hope that anything I create could be of worth. It is the very definition of existing instead of living. I think the same is true for many addictions. They are a substitution for the challenge of real things and real people. Real relationships involve delayed gratification that we often don't want to delay.

Count up the number of hours you spend in front of the TV in a week. During those hours you may not be learning very much, and you are probably not communicating meaningfully with friends or family. You may well be entertained, but you are, on the whole, not connecting with the broken

parts of our world where TV cameras may never go.

The writer Tom Wright once surprised himself when he worked out that he spent one day of his life every year brushing his teeth! Work it out. Two minutes in the morning plus two minutes in the evening, then do the sums. Incredible! It immediately made me think of how much time I spend watching TV in a day and therefore how much of my year I give over to it! We're talking weeks!

P.S. DOES ANYONE ELSE SING THE ACTORS' NAMES TO THE TUNE OF THE OPENING TITLES? ONCE YOU'VE TRIED IT, YOU'LL NEVER LOOK BACK

Thanks Lucie Shuker.

ADDICTIONS

I'm sitting where your
arms can reach me.
I could throw a stone to beauty.
Everyone who I love is here.
There's more than
ample stimulation,
No excuse for my frustration.
Still the box is pulling me near.

Addictions can come in
All shapes and sizes
Prediction – you're sucked in
by my intellectual disguises
I know it's a crazy, shallow thing
But just now I'd rather watch
'The West Wing'

The ringing phone
should stop fixation -
A living soul wants conversation,
But not a contest,
not even close.

So when does treat
become temptation?
When does rest
become stagnation?
Creative juices
now decompose.

Could this be my real life,
perhaps without the edits?
Just one more episode?
We could fast
forward the credits.

Words and Music: Andy Flannagan -
©2011 Downwardly Mobile Music

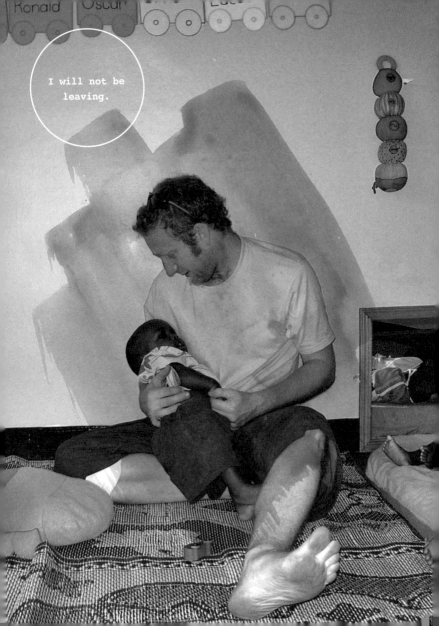

In 2007, I was in Uganda as part of a group running a kids club and investigating how we could support some of the amazing work going on out there.

It was a trip where I had already witnessed so much poverty and learnt so much about real joy. On the very last day we were brought to an amazing place called Sanyu baby orphanage. I had been to orphanages before, but the twelve months preceding this visit had included much precious time with Hannah, my niece. Through her I had become well aware of how a well-nurtured, well-loved, and well-held child interacts with their surroundings and particularly with others in the vicinity.

So it was traumatic to be introduced to the children of Sanyu. The contrast could not have been greater. These babies have been left on the streets of Kampala, sometimes in ditches, sometimes in toilets, either because their families have no resource left to care for them, or because they are unwanted. Some of them are left alone for days before they are discovered. The effects of this isolation were all too painfully visible. We were encouraged by the staff to spend some time "up close" with the kids, as any small

Heaven ○————————————————————————————

amount of contact can be helpful. A little guy called Joseph who was 18 months old caught my eye. He was covered in sweat and staring at the wall. I went to sit with him and then hold him. At no point did he make eye contact with me. When I put my finger into his little hand, expecting his tiny fingers to curl around mine, there was just no elasticity or response to my touch. Toys like jack-in-the-boxes that would have brought squeals of delight from my sister's kids brought squeals of fear from Joseph. It was so painful to see the indelible effects of the deprivation of love. You wondered how any of these kids would get by in life with this horrendous reverse headstart. I resolved to stay with Joseph until I saw some sign of him interacting with me. His fear was so palpable. Until being at the orphanage he

had never known anything but rejection and isolation. And there are so many just like him.

I stayed with him for less than an hour.

Then I left him too.

NEXT?

I got married to my wife Jen in June 2009. We decided that as independent adults we already had more than enough household stuff to be going on with. We also wanted to involve all our wedding guests in something bigger than the celebration which fleshed out its theme - the fusion of heaven and

Heaven seemed very separate to that painful and hopeless situation.

earth. So as we thought about our wedding list, the babies of Sanyu sprung back into my mind. *There was a home that really could do with some stocking.* So rather than our list having the usual kettle, bread maker, lean mean grilling machine and various other appliances that would sit unused for great chunks of their lives, our list had mattresses, cots, medicines and cleaning equipment. The response from our guests was incredible. In the end, the orphanage was able to buy £10,500 worth of new equipment. On the wedding day itself, we were able to encourage people that they had joined us on the journey of bringing some heaven to a very specific point on the earth. It was what I had cried out for that day in Kampala. Something had to change for this gorgeous yet bereft boy. Heaven seemed very separate to that painful and hopeless situation.

SPHERES

You might be thinking, "What do you mean by all this talk of heaven fusing with earth?" We might first have to define what we mean by heaven and earth. The problem is that many of us have a faulty cultural understanding of heaven, informed more by Dante and medieval art, than any sacred texts. Building on the dualism of Plato, where things of the flesh were 'profane' and things of the spirit were 'sacred', a comfort-bringing, but I believe incorrect understanding of heaven has emerged.

Nowhere in the Bible is heaven described as "where you go when you die". We have been sucked into images of clouds, white beards and harps. Jesus spoke about the Kingdom of Heaven as

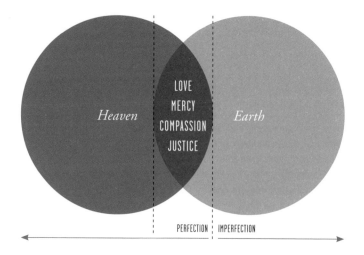

breaking in right now, and that it would find its final fulfilment at some future time. He prayed, "Your kingdom come, your will be done *on earth as it is in heaven*".I think a more helpful way to think about it is this. Imagine 2 spheres. One is the sphere of heaven, where things are perfect. The other is the earth, where sadly, as we all know, things are not always perfect. However, these spheres of existence are not separate. There is an intersection between these two worlds like the logo

for 'Mastercard' or those Venn diagrams from teenage maths classes. Every moment of justice, compassion, love and mercy sits in the intersection of those spheres. That is heaven on earth. Our lives are full of incredible moments, if we have eyes to see them, of those two spheres merging, when perfection trumps imperfection.

But there will be a point when the spheres of heaven and earth will fuse totally. The Bible calls that place 'the new heavens and new earth'. It is that incredible place of perfection where there is no more insecurity, racism, loneliness, computer viruses, worry, or death.

Michael Frost writes about how we often glibly imagine that magic dust is sprinkled on a couple during a wedding ceremony, bringing them to an instant unity. "Two become one", just like the Spice Girls tell us. I believe in the "one flesh" idea, but we all know (especially those who are married) that closer to the broader truth would be to say that two are becoming one. This is the gradual beautiful merging of husband and wife. It is a dynamic process, with moments of progress and regress just the fusion of heaven and earth. That is why we made it the theme of our wedding. The kicker is that incredibly we are called to be part

In fact, if that isn't the big picture, I'm not sure I want to be part of it.

of this fusion. I believe we are called to be partners with God in his big story of the restoration, redemption and reconciliation of all things to himself. If that isn't the big picture, I'm not sure I want to be part of it. Seeing the suffering of someone like Joseph and knowing how dislocated his future may be leaves me understanding the importance of this present existence not being the final chapter.

The difference this makes to how we live our lives is enormous. If we believe that our prime focus is to secure (and then help others to secure) an escape ticket for heaven, then caring for the environment, combating poverty or caring about all the other dimensions of someone's life will of course be less of a priority. If, however, we are looking forward to a day where all of creation is transformed and renewed, then all our actions, no matter how small and insignificant they may seem, become part of that huge process. We demonstrate the future hope by our actions now, bringing the future forward into the present. This is a vision that brings incredible motivation; because we know where we're headed, but we're not just sitting back passively waiting for it to happen, or pulling up the drawbridge to stay untarnished by a broken world. Instead, we are engaged in the world, active partners in seeing things change.

I pray that Joseph, wherever he is now, will know that future hope in his life. In addition I pray that he will experience heaven on earth right now. And I pray that all of us could see that those two things are connected.

I WILL NOT BE LEAVING

Barely breathing you lie,
Left hiding to die.
Starved start to a life.
No-one gave you a name,
They guessed your birthday.
Who counts your head?

Your loss is in my face.
Please meet my gaze.

I will not be leaving till
you hold my hand
I know that it's the
hardest thing to do
I am going nowhere
till you understand
That I'm not going to hurt you

Throwing toys to the floor,
Few get through the door

Fear bolts your heart.
Hands are weapons to you
Touch feels overdue
So rewind to the start.

Your arms lie limp at your side
From love denied.

How many more like
you are still in hiding?
How many more like
you are just surviving?
We need an army
To storm this front.
To reach for the broken
And touch the finger of God.

Words and Music: Andy Flannagan -
©2009 Downwardly Mobile Music

In November 2004, I had the privilege of visiting a fishing community just south of Chennai, on the south-eastern coast of India.

Times were hard because the fish stocks were decreasing, and there was no other useful employment in the vicinity. The beach itself was becoming more and more overcrowded with most of the community living in little set-to shacks vulnerable to any strong gust of wind. Our church were working with an amazing church in Chennai that was trying to help this impoverished community.

We had a wonderful afternoon playing in the warm Indian Ocean with the kids from the area. They loved surfing in on the incredible waves, but all they had were little rough rectangles of wood and plastic. No surfboards or body boards here. We gave this great little sport the moniker "Extreme Clipboarding". I remember being so happy, feeding off the infectious joy of these beautiful children.

They loved looking at the photos of themselves that I had been taking with my camera, and this revved up the competition to catch the next wave in the most artistic way possible. We left excited at the possibility of being involved in this community's future, especially with regard to improving their housing.

Fast forward to the 27th December. I am away on a writing retreat in a little cottage in a forest, just south of Gatwick. I get a phone call to say that three quarters of that community have been wiped out by the tsunami that wreaked havoc all over south-east Asia. My first reaction is, "You cannot be serious. We were with those guys just a month ago!" A distant problem was brought very close to home.

I cried and cried. I got my laptop out and clicked through the pictures and video clips of those beautiful children. The cruellest twist was that the same waves that had brought these kids so much joy were the same waves that had taken their lives. They would have been hopelessly exposed to the raging elements. I looked in particular at the picture of the massive Sikh temple that was the centre of their community, apparently half the size of Buckingham Palace. I had been told it was obliterated. More than anything, that brought home to me the scale of the devastation.

I know the official "line" on this. I know that as humans we are intricately connected to the rest of the created order.

So I know that when humanity went wrong, creation went wrong too, and therefore all is not as it should be. However, I also know that there is still a rhythm and a beauty about the created order now which makes certain events inevitable. The earth's crust has to renew itself, so the shifting of tectonic plates has to occur. These things I know. Further to that, my Dad was a biology teacher, so I have always been intrigued by the way that bacteria and fungi cause disease, but at the same time are absolutely necessary in the natural cycle of life and death in plants. Plants grow, then slowly die, being broken down by bacteria and fungi into nutrients that then replenish the soil to bring new growth. There is a natural rhythm to this cycle and endless others, which all involve loss and rebirth. These things I know but I was still left thinking that night in December, "I understand that creation in some ways has to be fragile, but does it have to be THIS fragile? This seems a bit ridiculous."

ZERO

The whole 'broken/fragile thing' doesn't just apply to the macro of the planet, but also the micro of my life. I don't know about you, but one of my primary frustrations in modern life is how much time I spend getting things fixed. Mobile phones, laptops, leaking roofs, washing machines and cars seem to constantly need some sort of attention. Added to this is the increasing amount of time it takes to keep my body healthy. The list of minor ailments calling for my care is increasing at a rapid rate. Then there are all the stretches and exercises I am meant to be doing every day to keep my neck, back and wrists in working order.

My frustration is that so much time is spent just getting myself into a fit state or appliances into a fit state to actually work. It inevitably takes up time in which I could be doing useful things. It feels like I am spending so much time just getting back to zero, never mind making progress beyond it. There are times when I am left internally screaming, "How much of my time do I spend just fixing broken things?"

Then one day I had the revelation that someone was simultaneously whispering to me: "That's what I spend ALL my time doing. You might say it's my job description – fixing broken things. Not a moment goes by when I am not restoring or reconciling someone or something within my creation, which has been painfully broken." It dawned on me that fixing broken things is not a frustrating necessity to get out of the way, before turning my attention to the real work, but that fixing broken things IS what we're here to do.

This reconstruction and renovation of ourselves and the planet is part of being human. Perhaps in the midst of the fixing I actually get a more accurate picture of humanity and come closer to the broken heart of a God who has all this brokenness in his face day-in, day-out. And who didn't avoid it when on earth. Perhaps I am getting some of my self-important Messianic edges rubbed off. Perhaps in getting to know all this brokenness, I am actually getting fixed myself.

SO, "FRAGILE" IS MY PSALM OF COMPLAINT WHICH I WROTE THAT NIGHT. AN INTERESTING REALISATION, THOUGH, HAD APPEARED BY THE END OF THE SONG, AS YOU'LL HEAR.

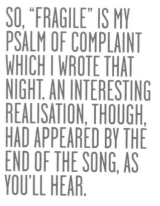

FRAGILE

Why does life have
to be this fragile?
Why is there a death
so close to birth?
Why does life have
to be this fragile?
Here on earth.

The same waves that
brought you
crashing in with joy,
The same waves left your
universe destroyed.
The same sand that once
warmed this white man's toes,
It makes graves for your
silent flesh and bone.
Smiles that I will not forget,
Joy that left me in your debt.

The same nets that once
put food upon your plate,
They lie cast like the die
that sealed your fate.

Reason here has lost its rhyme
And words feel empty
at this time

The same man that the winds
and waves obeyed,
Is the same man who was the
first one to know pain.
This same man, He could keep
control of everything,
But this same man knows
more than me about suffering.
So calm this
overwhelming force
'Cos earth and heaven
seem divorced.

Words and Music: Andy Flannagan -
©2005 Daybreak Music Ltd.

WHOLE

Something happened to me last summer. It was a relatively new experience. I was genuinely sad.

"Welcome to the real world", I hear you cry. I had become pretty stressed about an event I was working on. Various things had gone wrong, and more importantly for me, some relationships were out of kilter. I lay awake at night thinking incessantly about things. I also woke early in the morning. It was as if the negativity wanted to plant itself in my day before I had a chance to recalibrate to some truth. It neutered me. I retreated to making safe decisions to avoid conflict or excessive challenge. What was happening was no worse than any of the other challenges I have faced during my life. What was different was the creaking state of my soul and spirit. As I sat face-to-face with my none-too-

impressive coping mechanisms, I could see more clearly how much of me was broken and how "Work in progress" would be a useful sign for me to wear. We are all broken. The sooner we can admit it the better. It has taken me far too long.

We're all just biscuits who look good on the outside with our bold and shiny wrapping, but as soon some pressure is applied we can so easily crumble. If my crumbs have ever made a mess of your couch then I'm sorry. Who told us that the goal of life was to be self-sufficient, putting on a brave face to the world, impressing others into wanting to be our friends? There was a moment when the depth of my need of an embrace, of my insignificance, and then also my significance all crashed into me at once. The highlight of the week during my childhood was a Saturday afternoon. My Dad would come into the house and say, "Andrew, could you come and help me wash the car?" I would swell with pride because MY Dad needed MY help to wash HIS car. There was a flurry of excitement involving a yellow mac, buckets and sponges. Even the thought of being covered in soapy suds was quite fantastic.

This remained a wonderful memory for me until a few years ago when I heard someone else talking about washing their car with their son the previous day. "It was a nightmare!" he confided. "He kicked over the bucket of water, he got a stone in the sponge and scraped the paintwork, and he couldn't actually get rid of the dirt." A sudden realisation pulled the carpet out from under my whole worldview! My presence must have

almost certainly lengthened the whole process, and my sections of the car definitely didn't get washed as well as my Dad's! So I was left there stunned and bereft, wondering, "Then why did my Dad ask for my help?" Slowly, I came to the undeniable and beautiful conclusion that it was because he simply wanted me to be where he was.

HE WANTED ME TO BE DOING WHAT HE WAS DOING. HE WANTED TO GET TO KNOW ME BETTER IN THE MIDST OF A SHARED TASK.

Many people like me flit around believing that God needs our help to save the world, when a Father is very simply asking us to be getting up to what he's already up to. All over the world

This is the story of a good dad - a true father who brings genuine wholeness, in stark contrast to the 'gods' we latch on to in the midst of our brokenness.

I believe He is healing the sick, restoring the broken and releasing the oppressed. He doesn't need our help, but he wants our help. Unbelievably we are asked to be his partners in washing the car of his broken world with him. It's in the midst of that process that we get some perspective on our issues, as we recognise the needs of others. It's in the midst of that process that we draw close to the broken, beating heart of God for a world that is so often in pain. A gradual transplant occurs which means we start to respond to brokenness with the tears and empathy of fellow fractured souls rather than the frustration and impatience of those who still get their self-esteem from feeling more sorted than "the others". It's in the midst of that process that I believe we quite simply meet Jesus in the hands, eyes, and faces of the needy, marginalised, dispossessed, lonely, depressed and soullessly rich of our world. He himself said, "Inasmuch as you have done it to the least of my brethren, you have done it unto me." I believe meeting, working and learning with him is the only way any of us truly become whole. This revelation of relationship removes the rigorous rigidity of an attachment to God through mere religion.

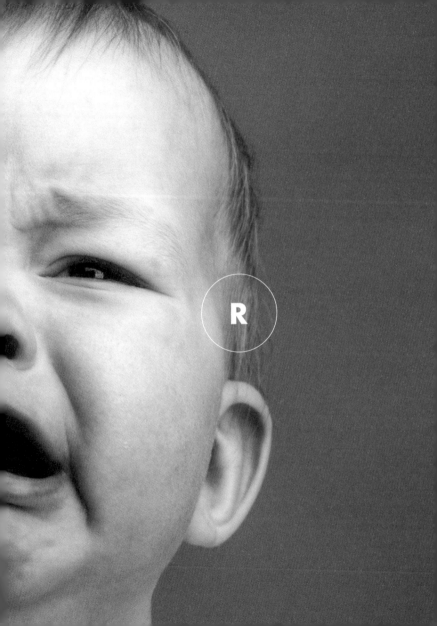

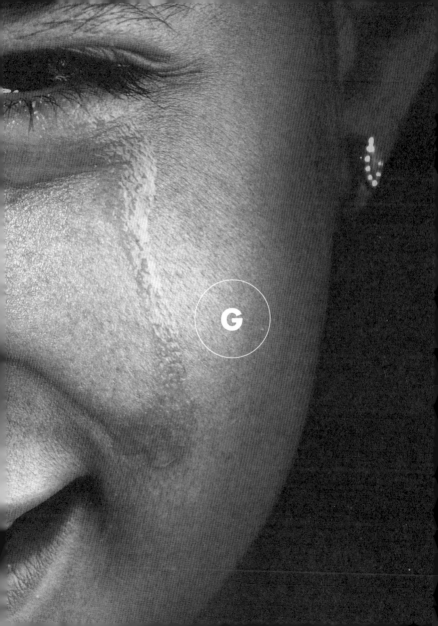

WE KNOW THAT THERE MUST BE SOMETHING MORE. SOMETHING BEYOND. SOMETHING BETTER.

It is wired into our DNA. Crying makes no sense unless there is something better that you are crying for. Crying affirms that something is wrong. Tears express a knowing that this is not all there is. Screaming out in pain makes no sense unless something in you knows that your present experience is not the way it should be and is not the way things will always be. The ancient scriptures put it this way, "He has also set eternity in the hearts of men." Our bodies register pain when things are not the way they should be. It's a good thing that they do. It's a warning sign, (especially if you leave your hand too near a frying pan). Pain has no point unless it points to a departure from wholeness. However, to depart from 'the norm' means there

has to be a normal. We would all admit that we are not whole. Some of us, however, can't admit or face that there could be such a thing as "whole" – that there is the possibility of wholeness. Our bodies and unconscious selves join with a broken creation that groans for it too. I believe wholeheartedly in that future reality, but I also see it breaking into our present in moments of justice and compassion.

So this is not a wholeness for which we wait passively and pathetically. We are ridiculously called to be partners in this project of the restoration, redemption and reconciliation of all things to their creator.

IT MAY TAKE A WHILE, BUT THE CAR DOES GET WASHED.

WHOLE

I am hoping you are near
I am holding back the tears

I am losing hours of sleep
I am swimming way too deep

This old world has
taken its toll
Whole

Longing to be whole

Saying no saying no saying no

Who will I be when no one else
can see?

Words: Andy Flannagan, Music: Andy
Flannagan, Alan Branch, Dave Cooke
©2011 Downwardly Mobile Music

When I was in my twenties, I was always in a rush.

Subliminally I think I believed I needed to achieve a whole set of things before I was thirty to make an impact on the world. The things that I wanted to achieve were good things. They mostly weren't for my benefit (though the motivations behind them veered from selfless to selfish, like a metronome.)

Then one day lying in bed, aged thirty-one, I had a revelation. It really didn't matter whether I achieved what I was thinking about by the age of 32 or 37. What was the difference in the big scheme of things? Thirty-seven would still be in my thirties, and somehow it just didn't seem to matter as much. For the first time in my life I was choosing between doing it slowly and well, or doing it fast to inject some sense of completion into my frail psyche. I am not saying that I always choose right now, but at least I am aware there is often that choice to be made.

Around the time of my epiphany, I was talking to someone who had just returned from a vineyard in France. They told me about how the expert vine-dressers know exactly which grapes to pull from a vine at different stages. The first grapes pulled go off to make £3 a bottle supermarket plonk. They need to be gone so that the good grapes that will eventually become the vintage wine can get exclusive use of all the sun and nutrients from the soil. With regard to my writing, or songs, or relationships, or anything, it made me think about how often I chose to produce the quick, cheap stuff rather than the good stuff.

The writer Gordon McDonald once assessed the long-term impact of leaders in a large survey. He looked at many folks who had initiated projects, programmes, businesses, movements, and ideas and whether or not their efforts had long-term impact after the event. He wanted to see if sustained transformation had occurred in their spheres. He came across plenty of big ideas that had made huge media noise but not led to long-term change.

Here, I summarise and paraphrase his findings via my good friend Dave Steell who heard it from the horse's mouth! He said that basically you achieve nothing

As generalised by Dave Steel

20'S
YOU ACHIEVE NOTHING OF ETERNAL VALUE

30'S
YOU MAKE YOUR MISTAKES

40'S
YOU START TO GET A PROPER SENSE OF WHY YOU ARE ON THE PLANET

50'S
YOU HAVE SIGNIFICANT LONG-TERM IMPACT AND YOU ENJOY DOING IT

60'S
YOU POSITIVELY REFLECT

of eternal value in your twenties. (Obviously he was generalising). He said that in your thirties, you make your mistakes, while in your forties you start to get a proper sense of why you are on the planet. He then said that in your fifties you have significant long-term impact and you enjoy doing it, leaving you to positively reflect during your sixties! How incredibly sobering, but also freeing! When you think about folks like Gandhi or Mother Theresa you start to realise the deep truth of this. I meet so many people who are so driven, and I recognise the way I used to be too. We find noble projects to be involved in that make a contribution to the world, but we know that there is an unhealthy drive in us that is simply crying for significance, status and the applause of our peers.

How wonderful it would be to be able to see life as a marathon, not a sprint, where the journey is as important as the destination. On a marathon, you can actually get to know your fellow runners, bringing companionship and mutual encouragement to each other. Compare that to the intensity of a sprint, where it is winner takes all, eyes straight ahead.

Even a glance toward your competition could be the difference between first and second. The old African proverb begins to make a lot of sense – "If you want to go fast, go it alone. If you want to go far, go together." For me here, there are echoes of the story of the Prodigal Son, where the elder brother was so busy working around his father's house, he forgot to stop and enjoy the beauty and privilege of his father's presence. He was working to gain his father's love. All he had to do was down tools, come to the party and realise that he already had it.

Some of us say we believe that we are unconditionally loved, but often our lives give away the fact that we don't really believe that. Anyone carrying out an audit on our lives might conclude that we are mostly trying to prove ourselves worthy of that love. This is especially true when we haven't experienced it in our natural families. And it isn't surprising. Everything else around us also screams the opposite of the truth. People can love us for as long as we make them laugh, for as long as they find us attractive, for as long as they find us interesting, and then drop us.

WHEN WAS THE LAST TIME YOU STOPPED FOR LONG ENOUGH TO JUST LET YOURSELF BE LOVED?

I GUESS THIS SONG SPRANG FROM ONE OF THOSE RARE MOMENTS. I HOPE THESE SONGS AND THESE STORIES HAVE PROVIDED A FEW FOR YOU.

FALL

I'll wait for the words
I long to hear.
I'll reach for the arms
that pull me near.
I'll hold on till all
the pain has gone,
Then I'll fall down
at your feet.

I'll stand, though
I may not understand.
I'll sit, with my short
attention span.
I'll walk slow,
learning to say no,
Then I'll fall down
at your feet

It feels like I could
now go the extra mile
'Cos I'm seeing now

You bleed till there's
nothing left at all.
You need nothing
from me yet you call.
You scream loud
that I have made you proud,
So I'll fall down at your feet.

There's a long road ahead
And it's making me wonder
If it matters how
fast I get there?
I've been rushing ahead,
But it's getting me nowhere,
So am I a tortoise or a hare?

Words and Music: Andy Flannagan -
©2010 Downwardly Mobile Music